Lena Eckhoff

Ocarina Songbook

Christmas Songs

Lena Eckhoff
Ocarina Songbook, Christmas Songs

le.eckhoff@gmail.com

ISBN: 9781730818004

Preface

Dear ocarina players,

welcome to my collection of Christmas Classics arranged for easy ocarina in C (12 hole models).

All songs complete with lyrics and chord symbols for guitar, keyboard or piano accompaniment.

Large, easy-to-read ocarina tablature shows you exactly what to play and when to play it, making this book ideally suited for children and beginners. I also included guitar chord diagrams so you can play these songs together with others and have a really special Christmas time.

Wishing you a merry Christmas,
Lena

Contents

Go, tell it on the mountain

Go, tell it on the moun - tain

o - ver the hills and___ ev' - ry - where.___

Go, tell it on the moun - tain that

Je - sus Christ is born. When I was a

2. He made me a watchman upon the city wall,
   and if I am a Christian I am the least of all.

3. 'T was a lowly manger that Jesus Christ was born,
   the Lord sent down an angel that bright and glorious morn'.

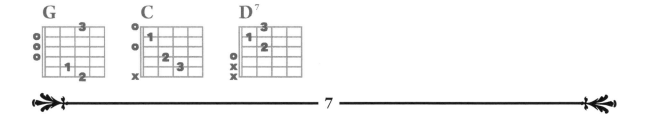

We wish you a merry christmas

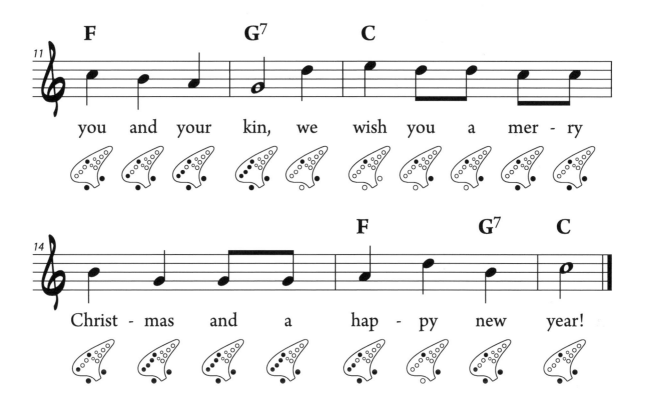

F | **G⁷** | **C**

you and your kin, we wish you a mer - ry

Christ - mas and a hap - py new year!

F | **G⁷** | **C**

2. Now bring us some figgy pudding (3x),
   and bring some out here!

3. For we all like figgy pudding,
   we all like figgy pudding (2x),
   so bring some out here!

4. And we won't go until we've got some,
   we won't go until we've got some (2x),
   so bring some out here!

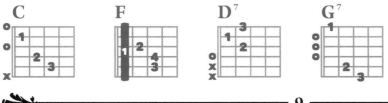

O come, all ye faithful

dore Him, O come, let us a - dore Him, O

come, let us a - dore Him, Christ the Lord.

2. O Sing, choirs of angels, sing in exultation,
   sing all that hear in heaven God's holy word.
   Give to our Father glory in the Highest;
   O come, let us adore Him, O come, let us adore Him,
   o come, let us adore Him, Christ the Lord.

3. All Hail! Lord, we greet Thee, born this happy morning,
   o Jesus! for evermore be Thy name adored.
   Word of the Father, now in flesh appearing;
   O come, let us adore Him, O come, let us adore Him,
   o come, let us adore Him, Christ the Lord.

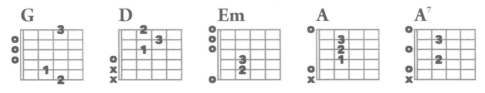

I saw three ships

2. And what was in those ships all three,
   on Christmas Day, on Christmas Day?
   And what was in those ships all three,
   on Christmas Day in the morning?

3. The Virgin Mary and Christ were there,
   on Christmas Day, on Christmas Day;
   The Virgin Mary and Christ were there,
   on Christmas Day in the morning.

4. Pray, wither sailed those ships all three,
   on Christmas Day, on Christmas Day;
   Pray, wither sailed those ships all three,
   on Christmas Day in the morning.

5. O they sailed into Bethlehem,
   on Christmas Day, on Christmas Day;
   O they sailed into Bethlehem,
   on Christmas Day in the morning.

6. And all the bells on earth shall ring,
   on Christmas Day, on Christmas Day;
   And all the bells on earth shall ring,
   on Christmas Day in the morning.

7. And all the Angels in Heaven shall sing,
   on Christmas Day, on Christmas Day;
   And all the angels in heaven shall sing,
   on Christmas Day in the morning.

8. And all the souls on earth shall sing,
   on Christmas Day, on Christmas Day;
   And all the souls on earth shall sing,
   on Christmas Day in the morning.

9. Then let us all rejoice again,
   on Christmas Day, on Christmas Day;
   Then let us all rejoice again,
   on Christmas Day in the morning.

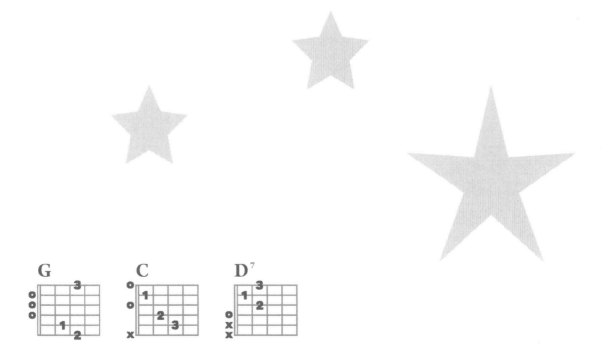

Angels from the realms of glory

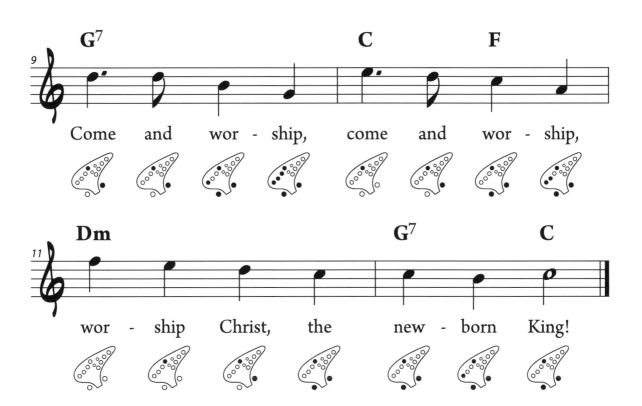

Come and wor - ship, come and wor - ship,

wor - ship Christ, the new - born King!

2. Shepherds, in the fields abiding,
watching o'er your flocks by night,
God with man is now residing,
yonder shines the infant Light;
Come and worship,
come and worship,
worship Christ, the newborn king!

3. Sages, leave your contemplations,
brighter visions beam afar,
seek the great desire of nations,
ye have seen His natal star;
Come and worship,
come and worship,
worship Christ, the newborn king!

4. Saints before the altar bending,
watching long in hope and fear,
suddenly the Lord, descending,
In His temple shall appear;
Come and worship,
come and worship,
worship Christ, the newborn king!

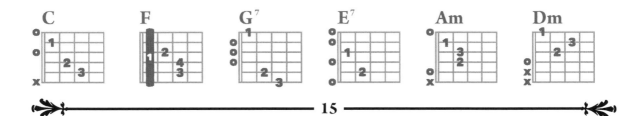

O come, little children

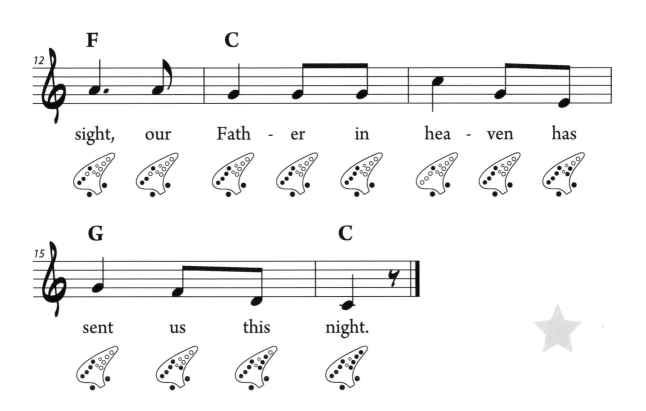

sight, our Fath - er in hea - ven has

sent us this night.

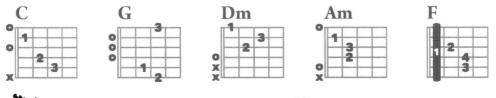

Jolly old Saint Nicholas

Jol - ly old Saint Nich - o - las, lean your ear this way. Don't you tell a sin - gle soul what I'm going to say. Christ - mas Eve is com - ing soon. Now, you dear old man,

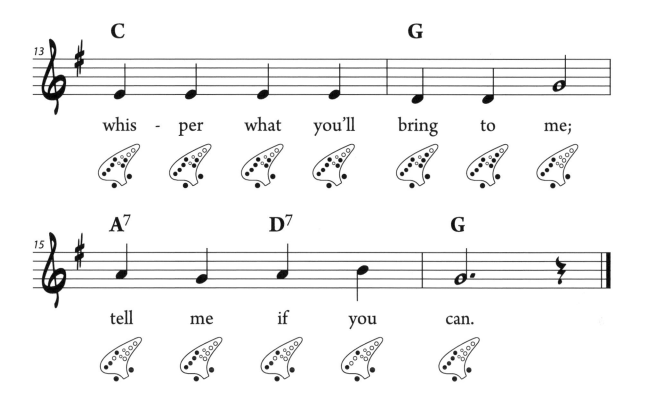

C **G**

whis - per what you'll bring to me;

A⁷ **D⁷** **G**

tell me if you can.

2. When the clock is striking twelve,
   when I'm fast asleep,
   down the chimney broad and black,
   with your pack you'll creep;
   All the stockings you will find
   hanging in a row;
   Mine will be the shortest one,
   you'll be sure to know.

3. Johnny wants a pair of skates;
   Susy wants a dolly;
   Nellie wants a story book;
   She thinks dolls are folly;
   As for me, my little brain
   isn't very bright;
   Choose for me, old Santa Claus,
   what you think is right.

G **B⁷** **Em** **C** **A⁷** **D⁷**

O come, o come, Emmanuel

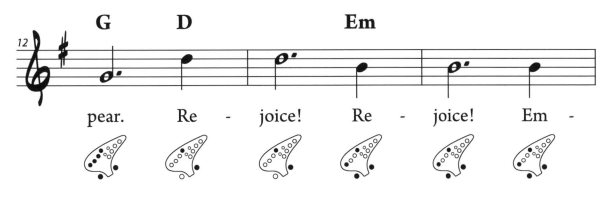

pear. Re - joice! Re - joice! Em -

man - u - el shall come to thee, O

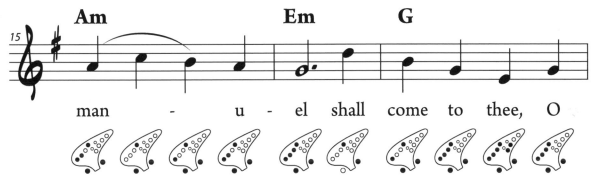

Is - ra - el.

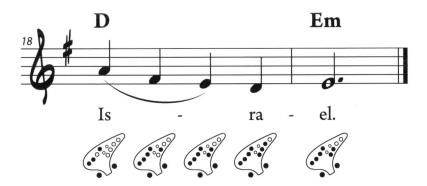

2. O come, Thou Rod of Jesse, free
   thine own from Satan's tyranny;
   From depths of hell Thy people save,
   and give them victory o'er the grave.
   Rejoice! Rejoice! Emmanuel
   shall come to thee, O Israel.

3. O come, Thou Dayspring, from on high,
   and cheer us by Thy drawing nigh;
   Disperse the gloomy clouds of night,
   and death's dark shadows put to flight.
   Rejoice! Rejoice! Emmanuel
   shall come to thee, O Israel.

4. O come, Thou Key of David, come
   and open wide our heav'nly home;
   Make safe the way that leads on high,
   and close the path to misery.
   Rejoice! Rejoice! Emmanuel
   shall come to thee, O Israel.

5. O come, Adonai, Lord of might,
   who to Thy tribes, on Sinai's height,
   in ancient times didst give the law
   in cloud and majesty and awe.
   Rejoice! Rejoice! Emmanuel
   shall come to thee, O Israel.

Good King Wenceslas

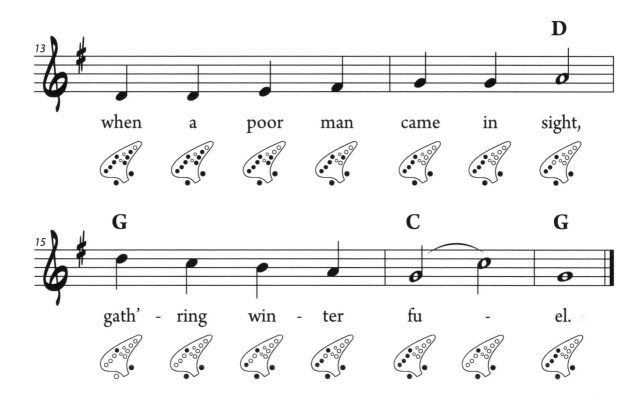

2. "Hither, page, and stand by me, if thou know'st it, telling,
yonder peasant, who is he? Where and what his dwelling?"
"Sire, he lives a good league hence, underneath the mountain;
Right against the forest fence, by Saint Agnes' fountain."

3. "Bring me flesh, and bring me wine, bring me pine logs hither:
Thou and I shall see him dine, when we bear them thither."
Page and monarch, forth they went, forth they went together;
Through the rude wind's wild lament and the bitter weather.

4. "Sire, the night is darker now, and the wind blows stronger;
Fails my heart, I know not how; I can go no longer."
"Mark my footsteps, good my page. Tread thou in them boldly
thou shalt find the winter's rage freeze thy blood less coldly."

5. In his master's steps he trod, where the snow lay dinted;
Heat was in the very sod which the saint had printed.
Therefore, Christian men, be sure, wealth or rank possessing,
ye who now will bless the poor, shall yourselves find blessing.

Angels we have heard on high

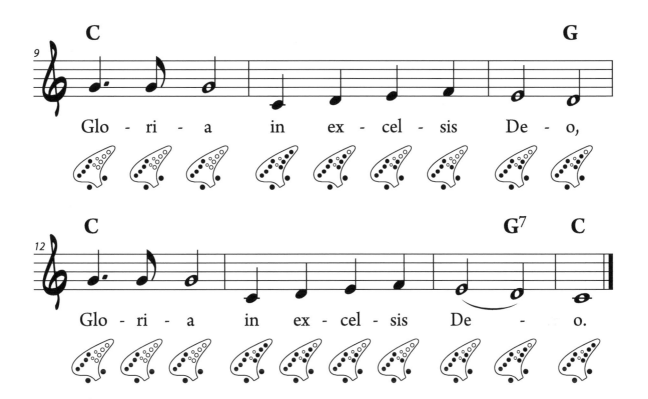

Glo - ri - a   in ex - cel - sis De - o,

Glo - ri - a   in ex - cel - sis De —   o.

2. Shepherds, why this Jubilee?
   Why your joyous strains prolong?
   What the gladsome tidings be
   which inspire your heavenly song?

3. Come to Bethlehem and see,
   Him whose birth the angels sing;
   Come, adore on bended knee
   Christ, the Lord, the newborn King!

4. See Him in a manger laid,
   Jesus, Lord of heaven and earth!
   Mary, Joseph, lend your aid,
   with us sing our Savior's birth.

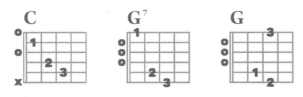

God rest you merry, gentlemen

stray: O _____ ti - dings of com - fort and

joy, com - fort and joy! O _____

ti - dings of com - fort and joy. _____

2. From God our heavenly Father,
   a blessed angel came,
   and unto certain shepherds
   brought tidings of the same,
   how that in Bethlehem was born
   the Son of God by name:
   O tidings ...

3. The shepherds at those tidings
   rejoiced much in mind,
   and left their flocks a-feeding
   in tempest, storm and wind,
   and went to Bethlehem straightway,
   this blessed Babe to find:
   O tidings ...

4. But when to Bethlehem they came,
   whereat this Infant lay,
   they found Him in a manger,
   where oxen feed on hay;
   His mother Mary kneeling,
   unto the Lord did pray:
   O tidings ..

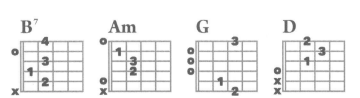

O holy night

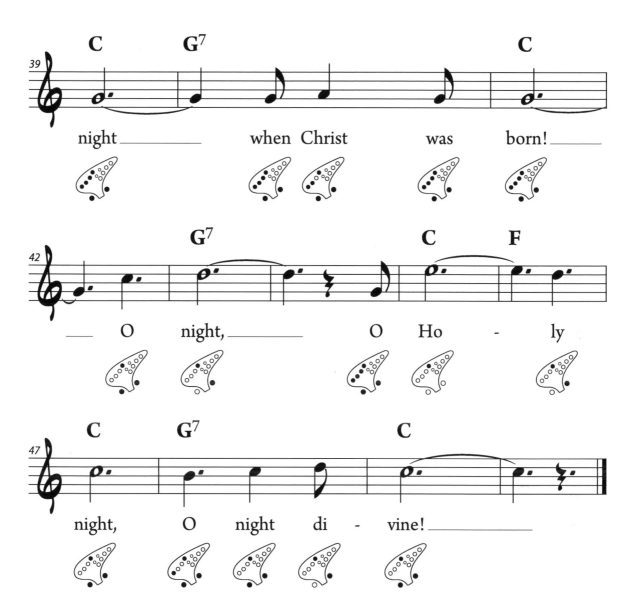

night _____ when Christ was born! _____

___ O night, _____ O Ho - ly

night, O night di - vine! _____

2. Led by the light of faith serenely beaming,
   with glowing hearts by His cradle we stand.
   O'er the world a star is sweetly gleaming,
   now come the wise men from out of the orient land.
   The King of kings lay in His lowly manger,
   in all our trials born to be our friends.
   He knows our need, our weakness is no stranger,
   behold your King! Before him lowly bend!

3. Truly He taught us to love one another,
   His law is love and His gospel is peace.
   Chains He shall break, for the slave is our brother,
   and in His name all oppression shall cease.
   Sweet hymns of joy in grateful chorus raise we,
   with all our hearts we praise His holy name.
   Christ is the Lord! Then ever, ever praise we,
   His power and glory ever more proclaim!

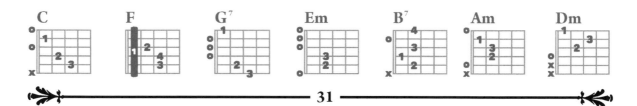

O Sanctissima

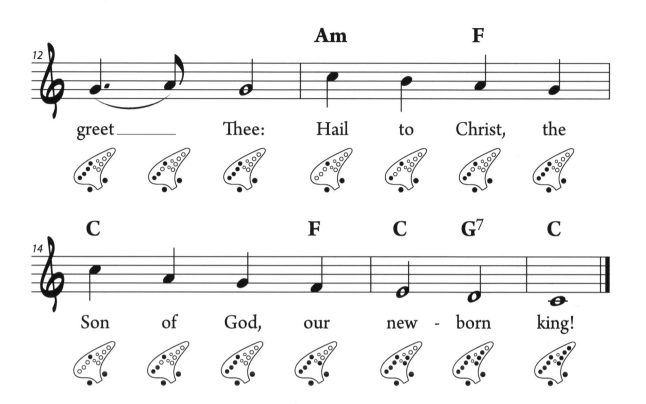

greet _____ Thee: Hail to Christ, the

Son of God, our new - born king!

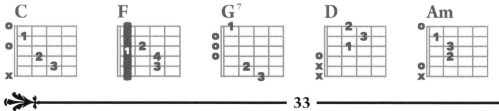

Infant holy, infant lowly

2. Flocks were sleeping, shepherds keeping,
   vigil till the morning new,
   saw the glory, heard the story,
   tidings of a gospel true.

Thus rejoicing, free from sorrow,
praises voicing, greet the morrow:
Christ the babe was born for you.

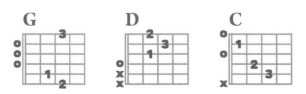

While shepherds watched

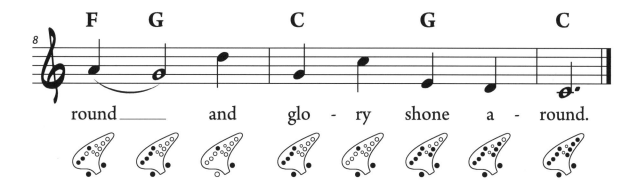

round _____ and glo - ry shone a - round.

2. "Fear not," he said
for mighty dread,
had seized their troubled minds;
"Glad tidings of great joy I bring,
to you and all mankind,
to you and all mankind."

3. "To you in David's
town this day,
is born of David's line;
the Savior who is Christ the Lord
and this shall be the sign,
and this shall be the sign."

4. "The heavenly Babe,
you there shall find,
to human view displayed;
And meanly wrapped in swathing bands,
and in a manger laid,
and in a manger laid."

5. Thus spake the seraph,
and forthwith,
appeared a shining throng.
Of angels praising God, who thus
addressed their joyful song,
addressed their joyful song.

6. "All glory be to
God on high,
and to the earth be peace;
Goodwill henceforth
from heaven to men,
begin and never cease
begin and never cease!"

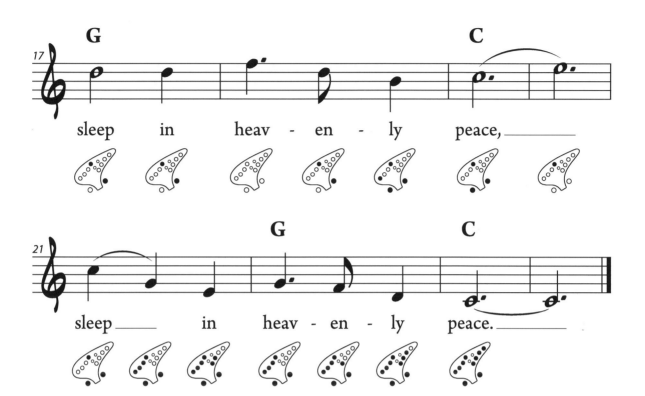

2. Silent night, holy night!
   Son of God, love's pure light.
   Radiant beams from thy holy face,
   with the dawn of redeeming grace.
   Jesus, Lord at Thy birth,
   Jesus, Lord at Thy birth.

3. Silent night, holy night!
   Shepherds quake at the sight.
   Glories stream from heaven above,
   heavenly hosts sing Hallelujah.
   Christ the savior is born,
   Christ the savior is born.

The boar's head carol

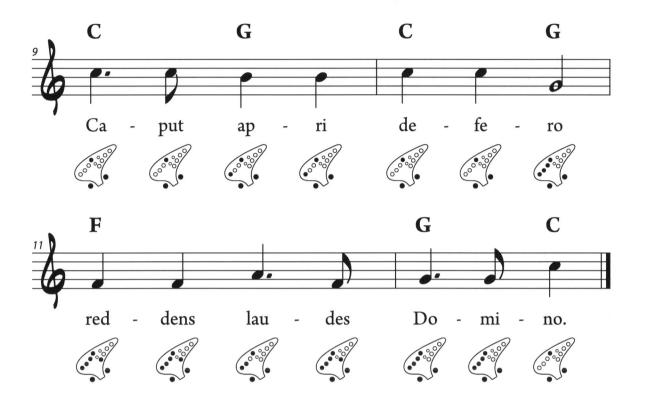

Ca - put ap - ri de - fe - ro

red - dens lau - des Do - mi - no.

2. The boar's head, as I understand,
   is the rarest dish in all this land,
   which thus bedeck'd with a gay garland,
   let us servire cantico.
   Caput apri defero,
   reddens laudes Domino.

3. Our steward hath provided this
   in honour of the King of Bliss,
   which on this day to be served is,
   in reginensi atrio.
   Caput apri defero,
   reddens laudes Domino.

In the bleak midwinter

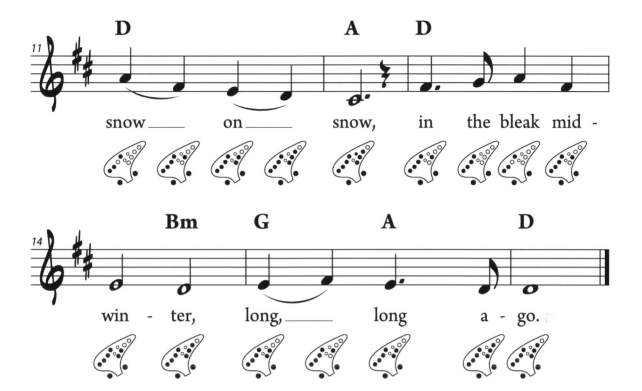

snow ___ on ___ snow, in the bleak mid - win - ter, long, ___ long a - go.

2. Our God, heaven cannot hold him,
   nor earth sustain;
   Heaven and earth shall flee away,
   when He comes to reign.
   In the bleak midwinter,
   a stable place sufficed,
   the Lord God incarnate,
   Jesus Christ.

3. Enough for him, whom Cherubim,
   worship night and day;
   A breast full of milk,
   and a manger full of hay.
   Enough for him, whom angels,
   fall down before,
   the ox and ass and camel,
   which adore.

4. Angels and archangels,
   may have gathered there;
   Cherubim and seraphim,
   thronged the air.
   But his mother only,
   in her maiden bliss,
   worshipped the beloved,
   with a kiss.

5. What can I give him,
   poor as I am?
   If I were a shepherd,
   I would bring a lamb.
   If I were a wise man,
   I would do my part,
   yet what I can I give Him –
   give my heart.

Joy to the world

2. Joy to the world, the savior reigns.
   Let men their songs employ.
   While fields and floods, rocks, hills, and plains,
   repeat the sounding joy,
   repeat the sounding joy,
   repeat, repeat the sounding joy.

3. No more let sin and sorrows grow,
   nor thorns infest the ground,
   He comes to make His blessings flow,
   far as the curse is found,
   far as the curse is found,
   far as, far as the curse is found.

4. He rules the world with truth and grace,
   and makes the nations prove,
   the glories of His righteousness,
   and wonders of His love,
   and wonders of His love,
   and wonders, wonders of His love.

Christ was born
on Christmas Day

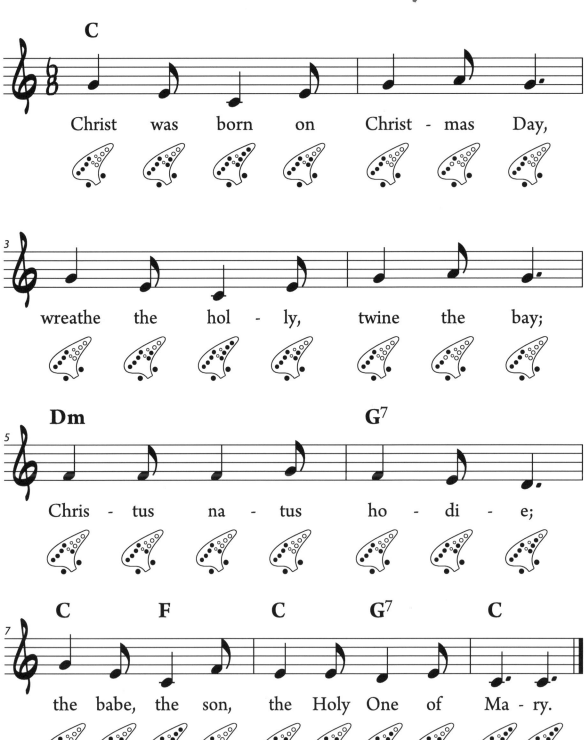

2. He is born to set us free,
   He is born our Lord to be.
   Ex Maria Virgine,
   The God, the Lord, by all adored forever.

3. Let the bright red berries glow,
   evr'ywhere in goodly show,
   Christus natus hodie;
   The Babe, the Son, the Holy One of Mary.

4. Christian men, rejoice and sing,
   'tis the birthday of a king.
   Ex Maria Virgine;
   The God, the Lord, by all adored forever.

5. Sing out with bliss,
   His name is this: Immanuel!
   As twas foretold in days of old,
   by Gabriel.

The friendly beasts

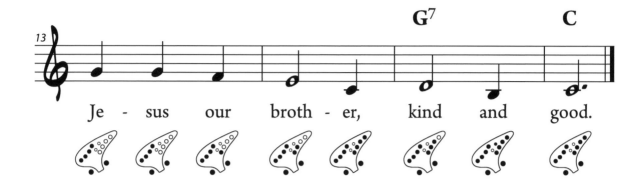

Je - sus our broth - er, kind and good.

2. "I," said the donkey, shaggy and brown,
   "I carried His mother up hill and down;
   I carried her safely to Bethlehem town."
   "I," said the donkey, shaggy and brown.

3. "I," said the cow all white and red
   "I gave Him my manger for His bed;
   I gave him my hay to pillow his head."
   "I," said the cow all white and red.

4. "I," said the sheep with curly horn,
   "I gave Him my wool for His blanket warm;
   He wore my coat on Christmas morn."
   "I," said the sheep with curly horn.

5. "I," said the dove from the rafters high,
   "I cooed Him to sleep so He would not cry;
   We cooed him to sleep, my mate and I."
   "I," said the dove from the rafters high.

6. Thus every beast by some good spell,
   In the stable dark was glad to tell;
   Of the gift he gave Immanuel,
   the gift he gave Immanuel.

7. "I," was glad to tell,
   of the gift he gave Immanuel,
   The gift he gave Immanuel,
   Jesus our brother, kind and good.

Still, still, still

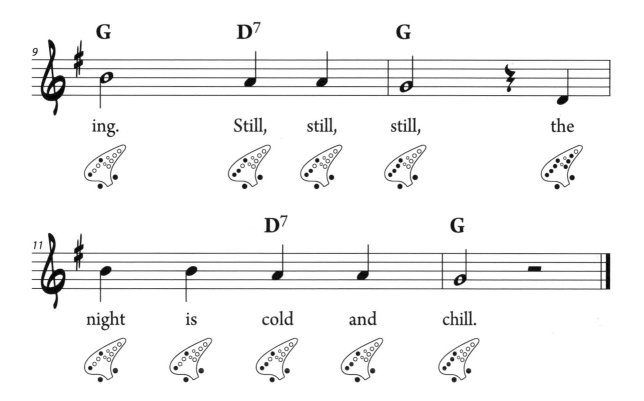

ing. Still, still, still, the

night is cold and chill.

2. Dream, dream, dream,
   He sleeps, the Savior King.
   While guardian angels watch beside Him,
   Mary tenderly will guide Him.
   Dream, dream, dream,
   He sleeps, the Savior King.

While by my sheep

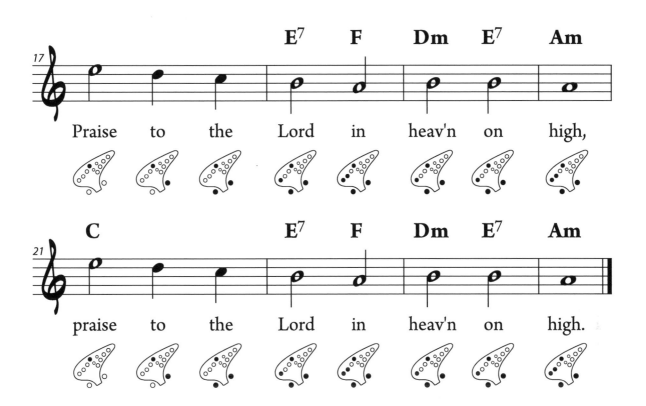

E⁷ F Dm E⁷ Am

Praise to the Lord in heav'n on high,

C E⁷ F Dm E⁷ Am

praise to the Lord in heav'n on high.

3. There shall the child lie in a stall,
   this child who shall redeem us all.
   How great our joy ...

4. This gift of God we'll cherish well,
   that ever joy our hearts shall fill.
   How great our joy ...

C   F   G   E⁷   Am   Dm

Up on the housetop

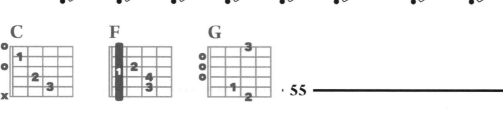

Over the river and through the woods

2. Over the river and through the woods,
to have a first-rate play;
Oh, hear the bells ring, „Ting-a-ling-ling!"
Hurrah for Thanksgiving Day!
Over the river and through the woods,
trot fast, my dapple gray!
Spring over the ground like a hunting hound!
For this is Thanksgiving day.

3. Over the river and through the woods,
and straight through the barnyard gate.
We seem to go extremely slow
it is so hard to wait!
Over the river and through the woods,
now Grandmother's cap I spy!
Hurrah for the fun! Is the pudding done?
Hurrah for the pumpkin pie!

Jingle Bells

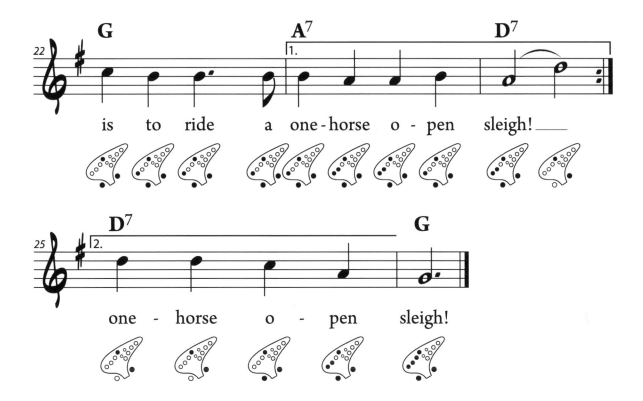

is to ride a one-horse o-pen sleigh! _____

one - horse o - pen sleigh!

2. A day or two ago I thought I'd take a ride,
   and soon Miss Fannie Bright was seated by my side.
   The horse was lean and lank, misfortune seemed his lot,
   he got into a drifted bank and we got upsot.

3. A day or two ago, The story I must tell
   I went out on the snow and on my back I fell.
   A gent was riding by in a one-horse open sleigh,
   he laughed as there I sprawling lay but quickly drove away.

4. Now the ground is white, go it while you're young,
   take the girls tonight and sing this sleighing song.
   Just get a bobtailed bay, two-forty for his speed,
   then hitch him to an open sleigh, and crack! You'll take the lead.

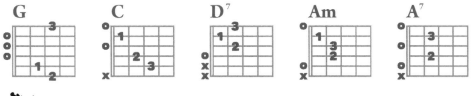

The first Noel

2. They looked up and saw a star,
   shining in the east beyond them far,
   and to the earth it gave great light,
   and so it continued both day and night.

3. And by the light of that same star
   three wise men came from country far,
   to seek for a king was their intent,
   and to follow the star wherever it went.

4. This star drew nigh to the northwest,
   o'er Bethlehem it took it rest,
   and there it did both stop and stay,
   right over the place where Jesus lay.

5. Then entered in those wise men three,
   fell reverently upon their knee,
   and offered there in His presence,
   their gold, and myrrh, and frankincense.

6. Then let us all with one accord
   sing praises to our heavenly Lord,
   that hath made heaven and earth of naught,
   and with His blood mankind hath bought.

C   **Am**   **G**   **F**   **Em**

Hark! The herald angels sing

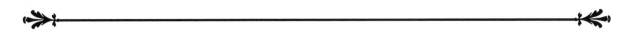

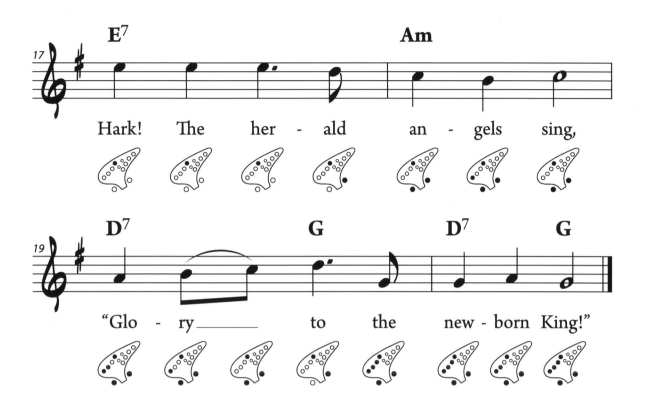

2. Christ by highest heav'n adored,
   Christ the everlasting Lord!
   Late in time behold Him come,
   offspring of a virgin's womb.
   Veiled in flesh the Godhead see,
   hail the incarnate deity!
   Pleased as man with man to dwell,
   Jesus, our Emmanuel,
   Hark! The herald angels sing,
   "Glory to the newborn king!"

3. Hail the heav'n-born prince of peace,
   hail the son of righteousness!
   Light and life to all He brings,
   Ris'n with healing in His wings.
   Mild He lays His glory by,
   born that man no more may die!
   Born to raise the sons of earth,
   born to give them second birth!
   Hark! The herald angels sing,
   "Glory to the newborn king!"

G   D⁷   D   A⁷   E⁷   Am

Deck the halls

2. See the blazing Yule before us,
   fa-la-la-la-la, la-la-la-la,
   strike the lamp and join the chorus,
   fa-la-la-la-la, la-la-la-la.
   Follow me in merry measure,
   fa-la-la-la-la, la-la-la-la,
   while I tell of yuletide treasure,
   fa-la-la-la-la, la-la-la-la.

3. Fast away the old year passes,
   fa-la-la-la-la, la-la-la-la,
   hail the new year, ye lads and lasses,
   fa-la-la-la-la, la-la-la-la.
   Sing we joyous all together,
   fa-la-la-la-la, la-la-la-la,
   heedless of the wind and weather,
   fa-la-la-la-la, la-la-la-la.

C   **G⁷**   **Am**   **Em**   **D⁷** **F**

It came upon a midnight clear

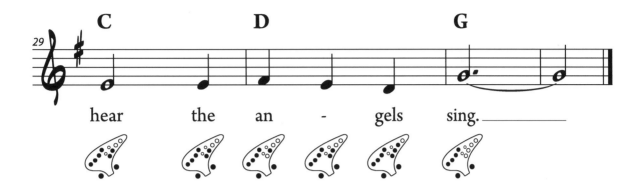

hear   the   an - gels   sing._____

2. Still through the cloven skies they come,
   with peaceful wings unfurled;
   And still their heavenly music floats,
   o'er all the weary world.
   Above its sad and lowly plains,
   they bend on hovering wing.
   And ever o'er its Babel sounds
   The blessed angels sing.

3. O ye beneath life's crushing load,
   whose forms are bending low;
   Who toil along the climbing way
   with painful steps and slow.
   Look now, for glad and golden hours
   come swiftly on the wing.
   Oh rest beside the weary road,
   and hear the angels sing.

4. For lo! the days are hastening on,
   by prophets seen of old;
   When with the ever-circling years,
   shall come the time foretold.
   When the new heaven and earth shall own,
   the prince of peace, their king.
   And the whole world send back the song,
   which now the angels sing.

Ding Dong! Merrily on high

2. E'en so here below, below,
   let steeple bells be swungen;
   And "Io, io, io!"
   by priest and people sungen.

3. Pray you, dutifully prime,
   your matin chime, ye ringers;
   May you beautifully rime
   your eventime song, ye singers.

G

C

D⁷

Em

Am

O Christmas tree

2. O Christmas tree, O Christmas tree,
   such pleasure do you bring me!
   O Christmas tree, = Christmas tree,
   such pleasure do you bring me!
   For every year this Christmas tree,
   brings to us such joy and glee.
   O Christmas tree, O Christmas tree,
   such pleasure do you bring me!

3. O Christmas tree, O Christmas tree,
   you'll ever be unchanging!
   A symbol of goodwill and love,
   you'll ever be unchanging!
   Each shining light each silver bell,
   no-one alive spreads cheer so well.
   O Christmas tree, O Christmas tree,
   You'll ever be unchanging.

He is born, the holy child

Chorus
He is born, the holy child,
play the oboe and bagpipes merrily!
He is born, the holy child,
sing we all of the Savior mild.

2. O how lovely, O how pure,
   is this perfect child of heaven;
   O how lovely, O how pure,
   gracious gift of God to man!
   He is born, the holy child …

3. Jesus, Lord of all the world,
   coming as a child among us,
   Jesus, Lord of all the world,
   grant to us Thy heavenly peace.
   He is born, the holy child …

G

D

C

Bring a torch, Jeanette, Isabella

2. Who is that, knocking on the door?
   Who is it, knocking like that?
   Open up, we've arranged on a platter,
   lovely cakes that we have brought here.
   Knock! Knock! Knock! Open the door for us!
   Knock! Knock! Knock! Let's celebrate!

3. It is wrong when the child is sleeping,
   it is wrong to talk so loud.
   Silence, now as you gather around,
   lest your noise should waken Jesus.
   Hush! Hush! see how He slumbers;
   Hush! Hush! see how fast He sleeps!

4. Softly now unto the stable,
   softly for a moment come!
   Look and see how charming is Jesus,
   look at him there, His cheeks are rosy!
   Hush! Hush! see how the Child is sleeping;
   Hush! Hush! see how he smiles in dreams!

G   **Em**   **Am**   **D**   **C**

Gather around the christmas tree

2. Gather around the Christmas tree!
   Gather around the Christmas tree!
   Once the pride of the mountainside,
   now cut down to grace our Christmastide;
   For Christ from heav'n to earth came down,
   To gain, through death, a nobler crown.
   Hosanna, Hosanna,
   Hosanna in the highest!

3. Gather around the Christmas tree!
   Gather around the Christmas tree!
   Every bough bears a burden now,
   they are gifts of love for us, we trow;
   For Christ is born, His love to show,
   and give good gifts to men below.
   Hosanna, Hosanna,
   Hosanna in the highest!

4. Farewell to thee, O Christmas tree!
   Farewell to thee, O Christmas tree!
   Twelve months o'er, we shall meet once
   more;
   Merry welcome singing, as of yore,
   for Christ now reigns, our Savior dear,
   and gives us Christmas every year!

G **D⁷** **Em** **Am** **Bm** **A⁷**

D **C**

Jesu, joy of man's desiring

2. Through the way where hope is guiding,
   hark, what peaceful music rings;
   Where the flock, in Thee confiding,
   drink of joy from deathless springs.
   Theirs is beauty's fairest pleasure;
   theirs is wisdom's holiest treasure.
   Thou dost ever lead Thine own,
   In the love of joys unknown.

Auld lang syne

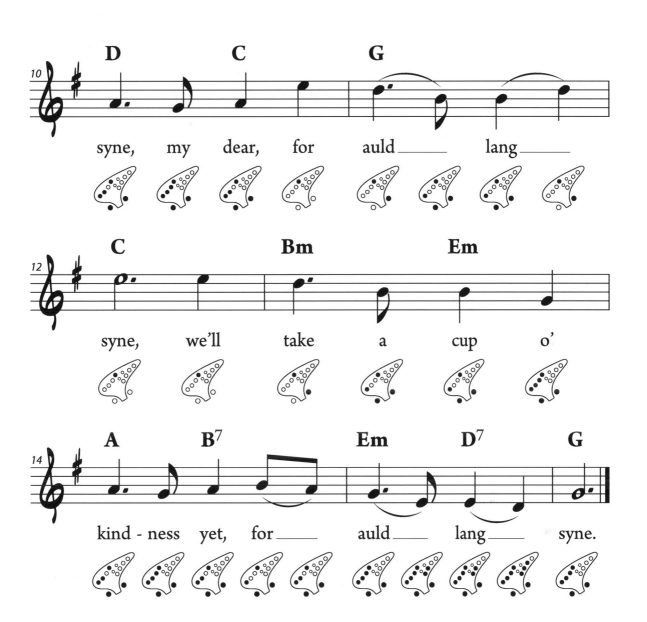

Chorus:
For auld lang syne, my dear,
for auld lang syne,
we'll take a cup o' kindness yet,
for auld lang syne.

2. And surely ye'll be your pint-stoup!
   and surely I'll be mine!
   And we'll tak' a cup o' kindness yet,
   for auld lang syne.

3. We twa hae run about the braes,
   and pou'd the gowans fine;
   But we've wander'd mony a weary fit,
   sin' auld lang syne.

4. We twa hae paidl'd in the burn,
   frae morning sun till dine;
   But seas between us braid hae roar'd
   sin' auld lang syne.

5. And there's a hand, my trusty fiere!
   and gie's a hand o' thine!
   And we'll tak' a right gude-willie waught,
   for auld lang syne.

G   **Em**   **Am**   **D**   **C**   **A**

D⁷   **Bm** 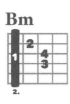 **B⁷**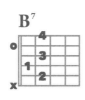

Wassail, wassail

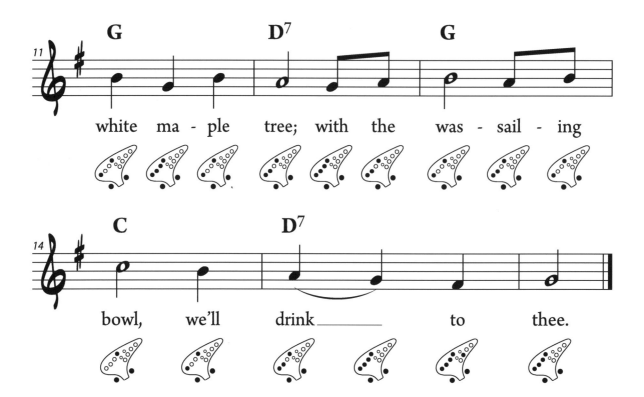

white ma - ple tree; with the was - sail - ing

bowl, we'll drink _____ to thee.

2. Here's to our horse, and to his right ear,
   God send our master a happy new year:
   A happy new year as e'er he did see,
   with my wassailing bowl I drink to thee.

3. So here is to Cherry and to his right cheek
   pray God send our master a good piece of beef
   and a good piece of beef that may we all see
   with the wassailing bowl, we'll drink to thee.

4. Here's to our mare, and to her right eye,
   God send our mistress a good Christmas pie;
   A good Christmas pie as e'er I did see,
   with my wassailing bowl I drink to thee.

5. So here is to Broad Mary and to her broad horn,
   may God send our master a good crop of corn,
   and a good crop of corn that may we all see,
   with the wassailing bowl, we'll drink to thee.

6. And here is to Fillpail and to her left ear,
   pray God send our master a happy New Year,
   and a happy New Year as e'er he did see,
   with the wassailing bowl, we'll drink to thee.

7. Here's to our cow, and to her long tail,
   God send our master us never may fail
   of a cup of good beer: I pray you draw near,
   and our jolly wassail it's then you shall hear.

8. Come butler, come fill us a bowl of the best,
   then we hope that your soul in heaven may rest,
   but if you do draw us a bowl of the small,
   then down shall go butler, bowl and all.

9. Be here any maids? I suppose here be some;
   Sure they will not let young men stand on the cold stone!
   Sing hey O, maids! Come trole back the pin,
   and the fairest maid in the house let us all in.

10. Then here's to the maid in the lily white smock,
    who tripped to the door and slipped back the lock,
    who tripped to the door and pulled back the pin,
    for to let these jolly wassailers in.

G

Em

D⁷

C

We three kings of Orient are

Chorus: O star of wonder, star of night,
             star with royal beauty bright,
             Westward leading, still proceeding,
             guide us to thy perfect light.

2. Born a King on Bethlehem's plain.
   Gold I bring to crown Him again,
   king forever, ceasing never,
   over us all to reign.

3. Frankincense to offer have I;
   incense owns a Deity nigh;
   prayer and praising, all men raising,
   worship Him, God most high.

4. Myrrh is mine, its bitter perfume
   breathes of life of gathering gloom.
   Sorrowing, sighing, bleeding, dying,
   sealed in the stone-cold tomb.

5. Glorious now behold Him arise;
   king and God and Sacrifice.
   Alleluia, Alleluia,
   earth to heav'n replies.

Em   **B⁷**   **D⁷** **G**   **C**

Here we come a-wassailing

2. Our wassail cup is made
   of the rosemary tree,
   and so is your beer
   of the best barley.
   Love and joy come to you ...

3. We are not daily beggars
   that beg from door to door;
   But we are neighbours' children,
   whom you have seen before.
   Love and joy come to you ...

4. Call up the butler of this house,
   put on his golden ring.
   Let him bring us up a glass of beer,
   and better we shall sing.
   Love and joy come to you ...

5. We have got a little purse
   of stretching leather skin;
   We want a little of your money
   to line it well within.
   Love and joy come to you ...

6. Bring us out a table
   and spread it with a cloth;
   Bring us out a mouldy cheese,
   and some of your Christmas loaf.
   Love and joy come to you ...

7. God bless the master of this house
   likewise the mistress too,
   and all the little children
   that round the table go.
   Love and joy come to you ...

D   A⁷   G   Em   B⁷

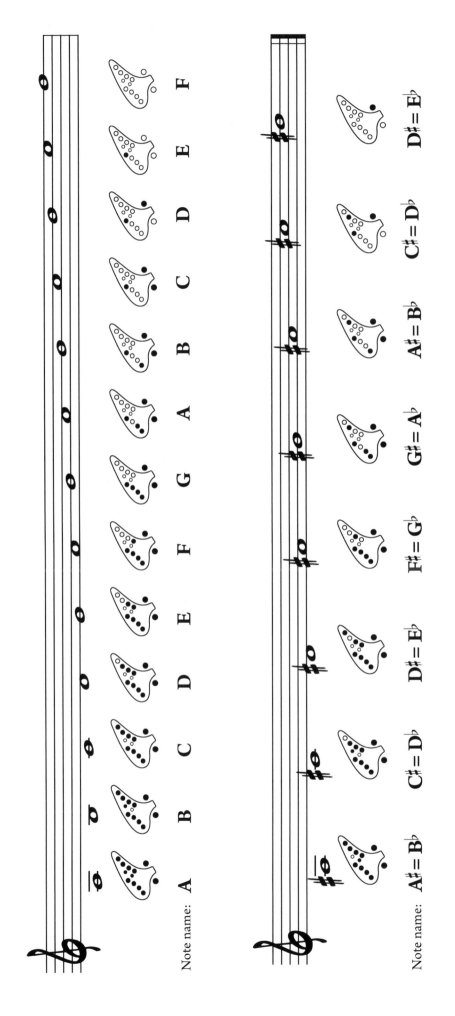

Made in the USA
Monee, IL
23 November 2021

82772290R00059